Green Tree Pythons as Pets

Caring For Your Green Tree Python

Green Tree Python breeding, where to buy, types, care, temperament, cost, health, handling, husbandry, diet, and much more included!

By Lolly Brown

Copyrights and Trademarks

All rights reserved. No part of this book may be reproduced or transformed in any form or by any means, graphic, electronic, or mechanical, including photocopying, recording, taping, or by any information storage retrieval system, without the written permission of the author.

This publication is Copyright ©2016 NRB Publishing, an imprint. Nevada. All products, graphics, publications, software and services mentioned and recommended in this publication are protected by trademarks. In such instance, all trademarks & copyright belong to the respective owners. For information consult www.NRBpublishing.com

Disclaimer and Legal Notice

This product is not legal, medical, or accounting advice and should not be interpreted in that manner. You need to do your own due-diligence to determine if the content of this product is right for you. While every attempt has been made to verify the information shared in this publication, neither the author, neither publisher, nor the affiliates assume any responsibility for errors, omissions or contrary interpretation of the subject matter herein. Any perceived slights to any specific person(s) or organization(s) are purely unintentional.

We have no control over the nature, content and availability of the web sites listed in this book. The inclusion of any web site links does not necessarily imply a recommendation or endorse the views expressed within them. We take no responsibility for, and will not be liable for, the websites being temporarily unavailable or being removed from the internet.

The accuracy and completeness of information provided herein and opinions stated herein are not guaranteed or warranted to produce any particular results, and the advice and strategies, contained herein may not be suitable for every individual. Neither the author nor the publisher shall be liable for any loss incurred as a consequence of the use and application, directly or indirectly, of any information presented in this work. This publication is designed to provide information in regard to the subject matter covered.

Neither the author nor the publisher assume any responsibility for any errors or omissions, nor do they represent or warrant that the ideas, information, actions, plans, suggestions contained in this book is in all cases accurate. It is the reader's responsibility to find advice before putting anything written in this book into practice. The information in this book is not intended to serve as legal, medical, or accounting advice.

Foreword

An increasing number of people are adding snakes and other reptiles to their choice of pets – and one of the most popular snakes is the Morelia Viridis, or more commonly known as the Green Tree Python.

Popular for its vivid and spectacular coloring, this python has thrived in captivity, as many breeders have also begun actively breeding and cultivating this species, oftentimes seeking to isolate and develop unique colors. Though not a recommended snake pet for beginners, the husbandry of Green Tree Pythons is pretty straightforward once you have the essential elements of habitat and feeding established. Some familiarity with this species and years of experience in handling and keeping other snakes is recommended before you set your sights on this gorgeous snake.

If you have ever considered adding the Green Tree Python to your collection of pet snakes, this book will provide you with essential information regarding this snak species. These pages also offer guidelines in recommended best practices of Green Tree Python husbandry.

Table of Contents

Introduction 1

    Glossary of Snake Terms 3

Chapter One: Understanding Green Tree Pythons 11

    Summary of Green Tree Python Facts 12

    Origin and Distribution 14

Chapter Two: Things to Know Before Getting a Green Tree Python 17

    Do You Need a License or a Permit? 19

    How Many Green Tree Pythons Should You Keep? 21

    Do Green Tree Pythons Get Along with Other Pets? 22

    How Much Does it Cost to Keep a Green Tree Python? ... 23

    What are the Pros and Cons of Green Tree Pythons? 26

Chapter Three: Purchasing Your Green Tree Python 29

    Where Can You Buy Green Tree Pythons? 31

    How to Choose a Reputable Green Python Breeder 33

    Tips for Selecting a Healthy Green Tree Python 36

Chapter Four: Caring for Your New Green Tree Python 39

    The Basics of Reptile Thermoregulation 40

    Green Tree Python Caging 42

    Heating Requirements 44

    Lighting Requirements 45

Maintaining Humidity 47
Useful Tools and Devices 47
Chapter Five: Meeting Your Green Tree Python's Nutritional Needs 49
Prey Items to Feed Green Tree Pythons 50
Feeding Fresh vs. Killed Prey 52
Tips for Feeding Your Green Tree Python 54
Possible Feeding Problems 56
Chapter Six: Green Tree Python Husbandry 57
Cleaning and Disinfecting the Snake Cage and Habitat ... 57
Tips for Bathing a Green Tree Python 61
Chapter Seven: Green Tree Python Handling and Temperament 63
Green Tree Python Temperament 64
Tips for Handling Your Green Tree Python 65
Behavioral Characteristics of the Green Tree Pythons 67
Chapter Eight: Breeding Your Green Tree Python 71
Sexing 72
Thermal Cycling and Cooling 74
Introduction and Mating 75
Ovulation and Pre-Lay Shed 76
Laying Eggs 77

Brooding or Incubation 78
Hatching 80
Chapter Nine: Keeping Your Green Tree Python Healthy .. 83
Respiratory Infections 85
Rectal Prolapse 86
Spinal Kinks 87
Tail-hanging 88
Necrotic Stomatitis 89
Parasites 89
Water Blisters 90
Green Tree Python Care Sheet 91
1.) Basic Green Tree Python Information 92
2.) Habitat Requirements 94
3.) Nutritional Needs 94
4.) Breeding Information 95
Index 97
Photo Credits 103
References 105

Introduction

While majority of pet owners may prefer the furry types of pets such as cats, dogs, or even mice and hamsters, a growing number of people are setting their sights on reptiles as pets – and this includes snakes.

Maybe not all people are the fuzzy-pet types. There are those who prefer snakes for pets because they are quiet, comparatively low maintenance, take up little room, and are interesting, beautiful, and elegant to look at. One should probably add that some people even desire the unique status that being a snake-owner gives them.

Introduction

But pet snakes being an uncommon phenomenon, and because of the many rather villainous archetypes that snakes have played in media and literature throughout the years, snake-keeping is passionately loved by some, and passionately derided by others. Some view snakes as loathsome, frightening, and dangerous, while others love, respect and admire these creatures. Snakes certainly do have a primal and dangerous side, and it should be stated here and now that one should not keep snakes as pets unless they are willing to understand what it means to care for one, and unless they are willing to take full responsibility for the animal's care and security. That means taking the time to read, research, and understand the commitment required to care for your pet snake.

If this is your first time to have a snake for a pet, then the Green Tree Python is perhaps not the right choice for you. This species needs specialized care, and the repercussions of a mistake can be severe. If you have had other pet snakes before, however, and are familiar with the kind of care and caution that is required in keeping a snake in your home, then this can be a beautiful and rewarding snake to have as a pet. Use this book as a guide and a handy reference, as well as a starting point for more information. Get a Green Tree Python as a pet only after you have familiarized yourself with the unique traits, temperament, and requirements of this species, and only if you are fairly

Introduction

confident that you have the time, the resources, the capability, and the energy for the long-term commitment required to care for this amazing and beautiful animal.

Glossary of Snake Terms

1.2.3. (Numbers with full stops) – The numbers are used to denote the number of a species, arranged according to sex, thus: male.female.unknown sex. In this case, one male, two females, and three of unknown sex.

Acclimation – Adjusting to a new environment or new conditions over a period of time.

Active range – The area of activity which can include hunting, seeking refuge, and finding a mate.

Ambient temperature – The overall temperature of the environment.

Amelanistic – Amel for short; without melanin, or without any black or brown coloration.

Anal Plate – A modified ventral scale that covers and protects the vent; sometimes a single plate, sometimes a divided plate.

Anerythristic – Anery for short; without any red coloration.

Aquatic – Lives in water.

Introduction

Arboreal – Lives in trees.

Betadine – An antiseptic that can be used to clean wounds in reptiles.

Bilateral – Where stripes, spots or markings are present on both sides of an animal.

Biotic – The living components of an environment.

Brille – A transparent scale above the eyes of snakes that allows them to see but also serves to protect the eyes at the same time. Also called Spectacle, and Ocular Scale.

Brumation – The equivalent of mammalian hibernation among reptiles.

Cannibalistic – Where an animal feeds on others of its own kind.

Caudocephalic Waves – The ripple-like contractions that move from the rear to the front of a snake's body.

CB – Captive Bred, or bred in captivity.

CH – Captive Hatched.

Cloaca – also Vent; a half-moon shaped opening for digestive waste disposal and sexual organs.

Cloacal Gaping – Indication of sexual receptivity of the female.

Introduction

Cloacal Gland – A gland at the base of the tail which emits foul smelling liquid as a defense mechanism; also called Anal Gland.

Clutch – A batch of eggs.

Constriction – The act of wrapping or coiling around a prey to subdue and kill it prior to eating.

Crepuscular – Active at twilight, usually from dusk to dawn.

Crypsis – Camouflage or concealing.

Diurnal – Active by day

Drop – To lay eggs or to bear live young.

Ectothermic – Cold-blooded. An animal that cannot regulate its own body temperature, but sources body heat from the surroundings.

Endemic – Indigenous to a specific region or area.

Estivation – Also Aestivation; a period of dormancy that usually occurs during the hot or dry seasons in order to escape the heat or to remain hydrated.

Faunarium (Faun) – A plastic enclosure with an air holed lid, usually used for small animals such as hatchling snakes, lizards, and insects.

Introduction

FK – Fresh Killed; a term usually used when feeding a rodent that is recently killed, and therefore still warm, to a pet snake.

Flexarium – A reptile enclosure that is mostly made from mesh screening, for species that require plenty of ventilation.

Fossorial – A burrowing species.

Fuzzy – For rodent prey, one that has just reached the stage of development where fur is starting to grow.

F/T – Frozen/thawed; used to refer to food items that are frozen but thawed before feeding to your pet.

Gestation – The period of development of an embryo within a female.

Gravid – The equivalent of pregnant in reptiles.

Glottis – A tube-like structure that projects from the lower jaw of a snake to facilitate ingestion of large food items.

Gut-loading – Feeding insects within 24 hours to a prey before they are fed to your pet, so that they pass on the nutritional benefits.

Hatchling – A newly hatched, or baby, reptile.

Hemipenes – Dual sex organs; common among male snakes.

Hemipenis – A single protrusion of a paired sexual organ; one half is used during copulation.

Introduction

Herps/Herpetiles – A collective name for reptile and amphibian species.

Herpetoculturist – A person who keeps and breeds reptiles in captivity.

Herpetologist – A person who studies ectothermic animals, sometimes also used for those who keeps reptiles.

Herpetology – The study of reptiles and amphibians.

Hide Box – A furnishing within a reptile cage that gives the animal a secure place to hide.

Hots – Venomous.

Husbandry – The daily care of a pet reptile.

Hygrometer – Used to measure humidity.

Impaction – A blockage in the digestive tract due to the swallowing of an object that cannot be digested or broken down.

Incubate – Maintaining eggs in conditions favorable for development and hatching.

Interstitial – The skin between scales.

Intromission – Also mating; when the male's hemipenis is inserted into the cloaca of the female.

Juvenile – Not yet adult; not of breedable age.

Introduction

LTC – Long Term Captive; or one that has been in captivity for more than six months.

MBD – Metabolic Bone Disease; occurs when reptiles lack sufficient calcium in their diet.

Morph – Color pattern

Musking – Secretion of a foul smelling liquid from its vent as a defense mechanism.

Oviparous – Egg-bearing.

Ovoviviparous – Eggs are retained inside the female's body until they hatch.

Pinkie – Newborn rodent.

Pip – The act of a hatchling snake to cut its way out of the egg using a special egg tooth.

PK – Pre-killed; a term used when live rodents are not fed to a snake.

Popping – The process by which the sex is determined among hatchlings.

Probing – The process by which the sex is determined among adults.

Regurgitation – Also Regurge; occurs when a snake regurgitates or brings out a half-digested meal.

Introduction

R.I. – Respiratory Infection; common condition among reptiles kept in poor conditions.

Serpentine Locomotion – The manner in which snakes move.

Sloughing – Shedding.

Sub-adult – Juvenile.

Substrate – The material lining the bottom of a reptile enclosure.

Stat – Short for Thermostat

Tag – Slang for a bite or being bitten

Terrarium – A reptile enclosure.

Thermo-regulation – The process by which cold-blooded animals regulate their body temperature by moving from hot to cold surroundings.

Vent – Cloaca

Vivarium – Glass-fronted enclosure

Viviparous – Gives birth to live young.

WC – Wild Caught.

Weaner – A sub-adult rodent.

Introduction

WF – Wild Farmed; refers to the collection of a pregnant female whose eggs or young were hatched or born in captivity.

Yearling – A year old.

Zoonosis – A disease that can be passed from animal to man.

Chapter One: Understanding Green Tree Pythons

Considered by many to be one of the most beautiful snakes in the world, the Morelia Viridis has captured the admiration and respect of many snake hobbyists and keepers all over the world.

More commonly called as Green Tree Pythons or Chondros (for a previously prevailing classification Chondropython), these snakes can go through a range of coloration during their lifetime – often starting out as either yellow or maroon, until later changing colors that can range from intense green, yellow, and blues.

They hail from three regions: Indonesia, Papua New Guinea, and Australia, though they have since thrived in

Chapter One: Understanding Green Tree Pythons

captivity elsewhere in the world, as snake hobbyists have actively bred and nurtured this species.

Although not an easy snake to keep – their habitat requirements are pretty particular – their husbandry is pretty straightforward once the essentials of environment and feeding have been established. They are generally not recommended as pet snakes for beginners, especially since mistakes can be lead to consequences that may be quite severe. Tree Green Pythons can sometimes be aggressive – and handling these beautiful snakes should be kept to a minimum. They are appreciated more for the visual spectacle they provide than for any close handling or tricks, but perhaps the inherent danger and equally stunning beauty are what makes them so popular and so well-loved.

Summary of Green Tree Python Facts

Kingdom: Animalia

Phylum: Chordata

Subphylum: Vertebrata

Class: Reptilia

Order: Squamata

Suborder: Serpentes

Chapter One: Understanding Green Tree Pythons

Family: Pythonidae

Genus: Morelia

Species: Morelia Viridis

Other Names: Morelia Viridis, Python viridis, Chondropython azureus, Chondropython pulcher, Chondropython viridis

Common Names: Green Tree Python, Chondro

Regions of Origin: Indonesia (Misool, Salawati, Aru Islands, Schouten Islands, and most of Western New Guinea), Papua New Guinea (Normanby Island, the d'Entrecasteaux Islands, and nearby island with a sea level of 1,800 m elevation), Australia (Queensland and Cape York Peninsula). In Florida, USA, it is considered an invasive species.

Primary Habitat: Rainforest areas

Description: A relatively slim body, a prehensile tail, and a large and clearly defined head. The snout is large and angular.

Length: 150-180 cm (4.9-59 ft) to 200 cm (6.6 ft)

Weight: 1,100 – 1,600 g (2.4 – 3.5 lb)

Color: Juveniles start out as yellow, red, or dark brow-black. Adult colors are primarily bright green, though some retain their bright yellow juvenile colors, while others turn blue. Breeding attempts have also resulted in a host of designer colors such as tricolors, high yellow, calicos, melanistic, true blue, and super blue. A recessive morph may also result in an albino.

Conservation Status: Classified by the IUCN as "Least Concern," but is included in Appendix II of CITES (Convention on International Trade in Endangered Species of Wild Fauna and Flora), where international trade is monitored and regulated.

Primary Behavioral Characteristics: Solitary, arboreal, nocturnal, and predatory constrictor

Health Conditions: Respiratory Infections, Rectal Prolapse, Spinal Kinks, Tail-hanging, Necrotic Stomatitis, Parasites, Water Blisters

Lifespan: average 20 to 35 years

Origin and Distribution

The Green Tree Python is endemic to New Guinea, Indonesia, and the Cape York Peninsula in Australia, and they are usually identified by their region of origin. Its natural habitat is typically within or near rainforests, in trees, forest regions and tall grasses. They are arboreal, which means that they live mostly in trees, though some of

Chapter One: Understanding Green Tree Pythons

them can also be found on the ground, in shrubs or in bushes.

This is not an endangered species, and is in fact thriving because of captive breeding. Most of the Green Tree Pythons available commercially are from Indonesia, where they have been bred in captivity for generations. By contrast, Australia prohibits the export of native species out of their country.

By law, Indonesia only allows the export of animals that are at least a second generation captive. Add that to active breeding efforts elsewhere where these snakes are exported, and the species has since flourished within captivity, thereby making them readily available for purchase or sale as a reptile pet – though they are still considered an advanced species in terms of care requirements and maintenance.

The first documented captive breeding of Tree Green Pythons are by Henri Kratzer from Switzerland in 1961. In the United States, the first person to successfully hatch green tree pythons was Karl Switak in 1973, from a gravid female collected from the wild. The first captive breeding in the U.S. was at Sedgwick County Zoo in 1976, while the first private hobbyist to breed this species was Trooper Walsh in 1977. The number of breeders have since grown, and they have worked tirelessly to enhance some of the vibrant and

Chapter One: Understanding Green Tree Pythons

more unusual colors – with amazing results. Some of the most extraordinary Green Tree Pythons today could trace their lineage back to some of the first successful breedings. Some are now considered designer colors, including tricolors, high yellow, calicos, melanistic, true blue, and super blue. Albino Green Tree Pythons are also known to exist.

Chapter Two: Things to Know Before Getting a Green Tree Python

In this chapter, we take a look at some of the more practical considerations that you would need to factor in before making the final decision to bring home a Green Tree Python. We cover such matters as costs, licensing requirements, and the feasibility of keeping more than one Green Tree Snake, or the feasibility of keeping them in the company of other snakes.

Chapter Two: Things to Know Before Getting a Green Tree Python

Before all that, you might first want to ask yourself why you want to keep a Green Tree Python as a pet. Green Tree Pythons can live for as long as 15 years, and by then, the novelty would have long worn off. If you are thinking of getting one of these snakes simply because you think it's a cool idea or because you want to be able to show them off to your circle of friends, then think again. Alongside the wonderfully exotic flair they can lend you and your home comes the responsibility of taking care of them. You will need to feed them, clean after them, spend for their care and maintenance, and educate yourself about the peculiarities of this species of snake. A mistake can be dangerous, not just in their potential aggression, or the diseases that they can pass on to humans, but because of the repercussions should they escape their enclosures. After several years, they will grow – which means that they will require more space and a bigger enclosure. And even after 15 years, they might never show you an ounce of affection.

Green Tree Pythons can be wonderful pets to keep – but they should be treated with respect, and this respect begins first with an educated decision about you and whether you can honestly say that you can be fully responsible for one of these magnificent creatures.

Chapter Two: Things to Know Before Getting a Green Tree Python

Do You Need a License or a Permit?

In the United States, there is no federal law governing private possession or ownership of exotic animals. You need to look closer to home – to your local and state laws and ordinances to see what is allowed and not allowed. The regulations vary: some ban or prohibit exotic or dangerous animals, while others require permits that set down requirements such as microchipping, an established relationship with a veterinarian, and even insurance. Some also require proof that you are acquiring the animal from a recognized breeder, and that the snake was bred in captivity (as opposed to captured from the wild). Permits may also be required for importing, exporting, or traveling with an exotic or a dangerous animal. This species is included in Appendix II of CITES (Convention on International Trade in Endangered Species of Wild Fauna and Flora), so international trade is monitored and regulated.

First of all, you have to check under which classification the Green Tree Python falls under – whether it is classified as an "exotic animal" or a "dangerous animal." Definitions vary, including the process for getting a permit, and so you really have to do your research. And you need to constantly update yourself regarding your local state laws at least once every six months. Regulations can change, and

Chapter Two: Things to Know Before Getting a Green Tree Python

you don't want to find yourself suddenly in violation of a law which was amended after you thought you had abided by it a year ago.

It is also a good idea to call your Fish and Wildlife Management Office. Also check the legality of keeping pet snakes based on the regulations of your city, town, neighborhood, and even your apartment building, if you live in an apartment. The simplest reason for this is that if you are ever found to be keeping such a pet illegally, the discovery could result in a penalty such as fines, and the confiscation of your pet. At the extreme, you might not be able to find a veterinarian willing to give your Green Tree Python medical care if you are keeping it without the proper permit.

If all this seems terribly complex, remember that you are bringing a potentially dangerous animal into a human community, so restrictions and limitations should be expected. It must also be added that the illegal trade in exotic animals is a lucrative business for backyard breeders and illegal importers. If you care about these animals at all, you shouldn't support activities which promote their illegal capture from the wild, or the breeding and transport of these animals in unsuitable and pitiless conditions.

Chapter Two: Things to Know Before Getting a Green Tree Python

How Many Green Tree Pythons Should You Keep?

It is recommended that you only begin keeping Green Tree Pythons after you have had at least three or more years of experience in keeping more docile snake species. You would need to be very particular and cautious in the care and maintenance of Green Tree Pythons, so it might be a good idea to start with snakes that are recommended for beginners at first.

As with most animals, the question of whether or not you can keep more than one Green Tree Python largely depends on your capacity – financial and time-wise – to care for them. To be on the safe side, you will probably need to keep them in separate enclosures – and this is especially true for juveniles and male adults, which can get quite aggressive with each other. While yearlings and adult females can possibly coexist peacefully with each other in the same enclosure, this is not necessarily always true as it would depend on the individual snakes. In any case, you should be prepared to feed your snakes separately, as feeding time can result in aggression between two Green Tree Snakes.

Even if you are keeping a reproductive pair together for purposes of breeding or mating, this does not necessarily mean that they should be housed together all the time.

Chapter Two: Things to Know Before Getting a Green Tree Python

Basically, keeping more than one Green Tree Snake requires separate enclosures at the least – ideally prepared beforehand, and these can be quite expensive. This also means double the effort of cleanup and cage maintenance. Assess your capacity to provide all these objectively, and be sure to make an informed and responsible decision on how many Green Tree Pythons you can keep.

Do Green Tree Pythons Get Along with Other Pets?

The Green Tree Python is a predatory snake, and this largely determines their behavior towards other animals, whether this is other reptiles or mammals. They can view other animals as either a potential threat, or a potential prey. While they may tolerate their keeper – particularly if they have been raised in captivity and have long since gotten used to human contact – this does not lessen their wild instincts, and you should not forget this if you are thinking of keeping a Green Tree Python for a pet. While they may seem docile and passive while young, this can easily change once your pet starts to mature.

The Green Tree Python is a wild animal that will never be completely tamed or domesticated – and while this may be one of the reasons some people get this snake species

Chapter Two: Things to Know Before Getting a Green Tree Python

for a pet, this fact also deserves to be respected and kept in mind at all times. You can do this by making sure that their enclosures are secure, and that your snake has no possible chance to escape. Keep this in mind, too, in your handling and care for your python. And equally important, make sure that your snake's enclosure is secure enough that other pets will not be able to open your python's cage. The same is true if you have children in the house – as children can often get into anything.

How Much Does it Cost to Keep a Green Tree Python?

The costs you will incur with a Green Tree Python pet does not stop with the purchase price – which can range from as low as $300 to as high as $3,500. Green Tree Pythons bred in captivity generally cost more than those that were caught in the wild – which is not recommended. Other factors which can influence the purchase price include the type, age, quality, and breeder. Better quality pythons from reputable breeders will cost more, but this is always better in the long run as you will have some assurance that the Green Tree Python you get has been bred in captivity, with the temperament of one that has been raised in familiar and low-stress surroundings, and is reasonably healthy. You can

Chapter Two: Things to Know Before Getting a Green Tree Python

always negotiate the price, and many reputable breeders might be willing enough to lower the price if they find you to be one who is truly dedicated to caring for this creature. You will probably find good quality Green Tree Pythons being sold by reputable breeders for less than $500, so there is really no need to buy the cheapest one you can find from a questionable source. Don't forget to factor in shipping costs, which can start from around $30 upwards.

As an alternative, you may also consider adopting a rescued Green Tree Python – though this is probably a feasible alternative only for those who have experience with this species. Yes, there are some that have been turned over to shelters or rescues by owners who no longer felt up to caring for these creatures, or were literally rescued after they have escaped from confinement. Some of them may require rehabilitation. Adopting one can cost around $250. You can certainly check your nearest animal rescue to see if they have any. Check out the following site that focuses exclusively on rescuing Green Tree Pythons:

Green Tree Python Rescue.
<http://greentreepython.org/adoptions.html>

Chapter Two: Things to Know Before Getting a Green Tree Python

Aside from the purchase price, perhaps the greatest expense you will require for your Green Tree Python is a well-provisioned enclosure – and this includes heating, lighting, substrate and decorations. Other costs include food – most often rats that would be sourced from a local breeder, veterinary checkups, insurance, and electricity costs for heating. Also factor in the costs of a permit or license – the fees of which are variable depending on the laws in your region or territory.

Though stated in rounded figures, you are probably looking at annual costs of around $720-965, broken down as follows:

Annual Costs for a Green Tree Python Snake	
Annual License or Permit Fees	$25-30
Veterinary Care	$100-125
Feeding	$50-200
Tank	$100
Lock-down top	$30
Heating bulb	$50-75
Electricity consumption	$300
Under Tank Heater	$25-30
Substrate	$15-25
Miscellaneous (water bowl, climbing branches, fake foliage, cleaning supplies, etc.)	$25-50
Total	$720-965

Chapter Two: Things to Know Before Getting a Green Tree Python

Remember, again, that these are just ballpark figures, and you will probably find cheaper alternatives in the market for some of the equipment you will need. On the other hand, upkeep will also be factored in: sometimes bulbs will need to be changed, and you will certainly need bigger tanks as the snake grows in size over time.

Some also recommend getting liability insurance just in case, as well as insurance for possible veterinary costs. Or you can simply set aside an emergency fund for those times when you need to bring your pet to a vet. If you're not getting insurance, it's a good idea to set aside a contingency fund of around $1,000 to 1,500 or more for unforeseen incidents like these.

What are the Pros and Cons of Green Tree Pythons?

Still not sure about whether a Green Tree Python is a good pet for you? Below are some of the pros and cons you might consider as you make your decision. We cover that which applies to pet snakes in general, as well as those factors that apply to the Green Tree Python in particular.

Chapter Two: Things to Know Before Getting a Green Tree Python

Pros for the Green Tree Python

- Provided you've done your research and took care with the set up of your enclosure, Green Tree Pythons aren't particularly difficult to keep
- A beautiful creature and magnificent to look at and admire, interesting to watch and observe.
- Comparatively more manageable than alternatives like the Emerald Tree Python – which though somewhat similar in appearance and coloring, are larger and more aggressive. Green Tree Pythons are more tame, and can grow up to 7 feet long.
- A good pet for allergy sufferers as they are do not carry dander and are therefore hypoallergenic.
- Hardy creatures that can survive many keeper mistakes that would kill most other pets. In fact, with well-informed husbandry that allows them to meet their needs and requirements, they can even thrive in captivity.
- A non-venomous species that is not considered to be endangered.

Cons for the Green Tree Python

- Providing their enclosure can be a bit tricky and expensive, and requires forethought and preparation before actually bringing them home.

Chapter Two: Things to Know Before Getting a Green Tree Python

- Can be quite temperamental and sometimes aggressive – not for first time snake owners.
- They have lots of long, sharp teeth – you should probably expect to be bitten at some point during your python's lifetime. The good news is that they aren't venomous.
- Entails the feeding of rodents – not for those who are squeamish. You will also probably have to set aside a special freezer to keep your Green Tree Python's food.
- It might be difficult – and even expensive – to find a veterinarian who works with reptiles and snakes.
- Can be carriers of disease such as salmonella that can pass on to humans – requires intensive and thorough cleaning of cages and enclosures, and proper sanitation of your hands, tools, and waste products.

Chapter Three: Purchasing Your Green Tree Python

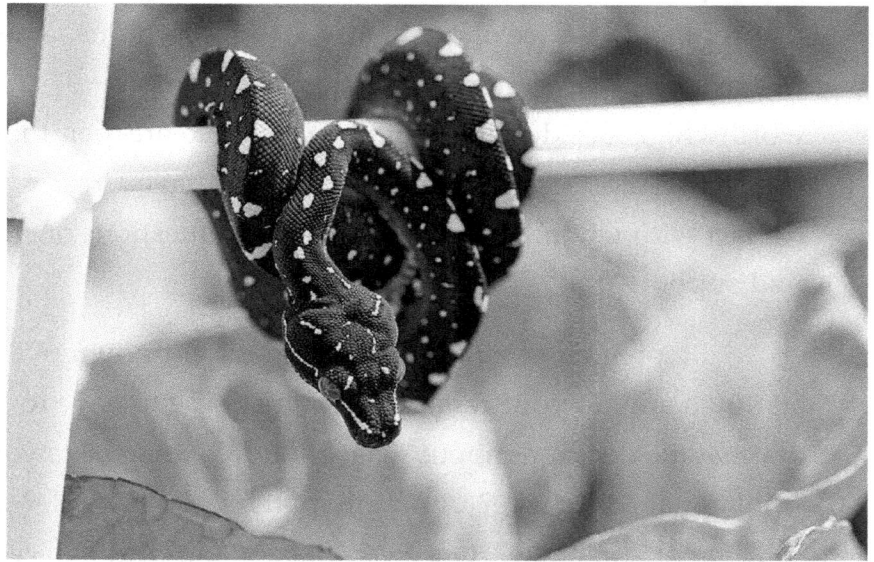

Now that you have become more acquainted with the peculiarities of the Green Tree Snake and the requirements for its upkeep, if you still desire to get one for a pet, you might be wondering how to go about purchasing or acquiring one.

You are going to have to devote some time to doing research and some legwork in finding a quality python from a reputable breeder. Don't just plunk down cash for the cheapest chondro you can find – with a dealer who is just as eager to get rid of his merchandise as you are of getting one.

Chapter Three: Purchasing Your Green Tree Snake

Not unless you want to end up with a Green Tree Python snake that comes with temperamental issues and a host of health problems. Be patient and take the time to really find that reputable source of quality Green Tree Pythons. This will make your experience with this species more worthwhile. Besides, if you find a reputable breeder, that connection alone is worth a lot as you will have a ready contact with whom you can network, ask questions of, and find support.

Before you even actually search for your own python, sit down and do your research. You're going to have to make some decisions about what chondros to get. Do you want a male or female? A mature python or a juvenile? A yearling or a neonate? Once you have made your choice, plan out and prepare their enclosures. This should already be set up before you even bring the snake home. Network and find a local breeder from whom you might be able to buy food for your Green Tree Python – whether this would be mature or juvenile rats, or pinkies. And last but not the least, find a veterinarian who has some experience dealing with reptiles. You will need all these support almost immediately once you acquire your Green Tree Python, so it pays to be prepared beforehand. Besides, finding these support systems readily available in your area will also enable you to assess your own readiness for keeping a Green Tree Python.

Chapter Three: Purchasing Your Green Tree Snake

Where Can You Buy Green Tree Pythons?

Finding a Green Tree Python for sale isn't as difficult as you might think – truth be told, there are breeders and sellers and retailers aplenty. Some of the ways by which you can find Green Tree Pythons for sale include:

- Looking for breeders and sellers online
- Going to a pet store
- Attending reptile shows

Many recommend purchasing directly from the breeder as this provides you with a competent source of information regarding the python's bloodline, lineage and husbandry. And since most breeders who enter this field do so because of a genuine passion for the creatures they breed, you will also find them to be quite knowledgeable about the species that they breed.

But the truth is that there are various factors to consider in choosing where to make your purchase, and while purchasing directly from a breeder does have its advantages, such advantages may not always be true for all breeders.

Chapter Three: Purchasing Your Green Tree Snake

For instance, breeders can range from small, private breeders to mass producers that supply large quantities of pet animals to retailers and pet stores. Sometimes large scale breeders may charge more because of the huge overhead they incur in their breeding processes, but sometimes small and private breeders may also charge quite a bit – especially if they are dealing with a particularly rare species.

Their willingness and availability to answer your questions is just as variable as the costs they may ultimately charge – regardless of the fact that you have skipped the middleman. Small breeders can be busy and may not always be available to answer your questions, but the same can also be true of large-scale breeders. On the other hand, pet stores may be closely connected or tied to a local breeder, and you may find their clerks or resource persons quite knowledgeable and willing to answer your questions as opposed to a private breeder. The same can also be true for those who join reptile shows, and you might find them truly passionate about the reptiles they are showing, as opposed to the breeder himself.

Don't discount a possible source until you have at least spoken to their point of contact, and decided whether or not you can trust them and are comfortable with them. How willing are they to answer your questions, and how informed are they about Green Tree Pythons and snakes in general, and about the python you are purchasing in

Chapter Three: Purchasing Your Green Tree Snake

particular? A good balance of their readiness to engage in a conversation with you and a good knowledge of pythons and the history of the specific chondro you are looking to purchase is a good starting point. Also balance this with the health of the actual pet you will be purchasing, of which more will be said later.

How to Choose a Reputable Green Python Breeder

If you have decided to cut out the middleman and go directly to the source, it pays to know how to choose a reputable breeder.

There are all kinds of breeders – some large scale, some with a more private and modest set up. There are those who have amazing and fact-filled websites online, where they also advertise their reptiles for sale. There are those who attend reptile shows, and there are those who opt to supply pet stores. How can you tell which is a reputable breeder?

Perhaps the best criteria you can rely on are positive feedback and review. In this case, networking can prove invaluable – whether online, in group forums, or within circles of hobbyists and the general consensus on the quality of a breeder's Green Tree Pythons.

Chapter Three: Purchasing Your Green Tree Snake

One does not become a reputable breeder overnight – it takes years of dedication, self-education and practical experience to become one. By the time one has established himself as a reputable breeder, he will usually have a number of satisfied customers who would be willing to vouch not only for his breeding processes, but also the quality of Green Tree Pythons he breeds. A referral from a veterinarian is no small thing, either.

It cannot be emphasized enough that you should know what snake you want to buy – what age, what type and what sex. Familiarize yourself with the requirements needed for the care of such a snake, and the unique temperament and behavioral characteristics of the specific species. Not only will this help you narrow down your list of breeders to those who specialize in breeding Green Tree Pythons, it will also enable you to ask intelligent and relevant questions, while avoiding such generalities as "Is this snake good for me?" Remember that Green Tree Pythons are considered appropriate for intermediate level snake keepers, not beginners. Not knowing what questions to ask would peg you as a beginner, who probably shouldn't be given responsibility for such an animal that requires specific conditions and care. A reputable breeder would be just as careful in screening out potential purchasers as you would be in screening breeders – especially if they are also offering a 30-day health and customer satisfaction

Chapter Three: Purchasing Your Green Tree Snake

warranty/guarantee. This kind of arrangement usually involves a warranty regarding the animal's health, and if they get sick or die within those 30 days, the breeder will either replace your pet with a comparable animal, or refund your money.

And finally, it is always a good idea to purchase locally than from a distant location. Why? Unless you are willing to travel a long distance to visit the breeder and to see his pythons, chances are that a long-distance purchase means that you might never even meet the breeder face-to-face, much less see the snake you are purchasing before it is shipped to you.

Sourcing from local breeders also allows you the possible advantage of being allowed a visit or a tour of their facilities. Whether large scale or small scale, what you are looking for is a clean, organized set up where the animals are well cared for. During such a visit, you can enter into a dialogue or conversation with the breeder, and finding one who is knowledgeable and willing to answer all your questions and concerns, as well as one you are comfortable with, is always a good sign. You will probably contact the breeder again within the first few weeks after you have made your purchase, to consult with him or ask questions, so a certain level of trust is always a good thing.

Chapter Three: Purchasing Your Green Tree Snake

Tips for Selecting a Healthy Green Tree Python

Once you have selected your breeder of choice, now it is time for you to select the Green Tree Python you will be bringing home.

Regardless of what age, sex, or size python you are looking for, you are looking for a healthy animal with no illnesses or diseases, and as much as possible, no temperamental issues that would make things difficult for you when it comes to general snake husbandry such as feeding or cleaning their cage.

Most experts recommend asking for a 30 day warranty wherein the breeder agrees to either replace or refund your money if the Green Tree Python gets sick or dies within 30 days after you have brought them home. A breeder who is confident in the health of the animals he breeds should be more than willing to do so, and an agreement regarding this would go a long way to establish trust between the both of you right from the beginning.

This 30 day warranty is important because it may not always be easy to tell whether a snake is sick or not. After all, most snakes don't really do anything by which you can tell if something is wrong or if they are sick – unlike with more common pets like dogs or cats. Snakes just remain still and watch you, or they ignore you. 30 days is more than a

Chapter Three: Purchasing Your Green Tree Snake

sufficient period to determine whether or not a Green Tree Python is reasonably healthy.

That said, watch out for possible signs of illness such as bubbles coming out of their nose, retained skin, closed eyes, and mouth rot.

It is also a good idea to ask for a feeding demonstration before finalizing your purchase. This way, you get to observe how the snake has been accustomed to feeding, and whether or not they have a good appetite. One of the things new Green Tree Python owners inevitably worry about is the refusal of their new pet to eat or feed. Make sure that they are eating well and has a healthy appetite before bringing them home – otherwise you might find yourself force-feeding your snake almost immediately after bringing them home.

Observing how the breeder and the snake react to each during feeding time will also enable you to judge a bit of the snake's temperament. If the snake is accustomed to slow and deliberate movements, for instance, this will guide you in future care and husbandry for your snake.

Chapter Three: Purchasing Your Green Tree Snake

Chapter Four: Caring for Your New Green Tree Python

Central to the care of your Green Tree Python is a proper set up of their habitat. What you will be doing is providing them with an environment in which they can thrive, and to do that, you need to emulate the conditions of their natural habitat as much as possible.

The main habitat of Green Tree Pythons in the wild are forested areas or rainforests. They are primarily arboreal, which means that they live in trees in which they rest in the branches. More often than not, you will find them in a resting or sleeping position in which they loop a coil or two over a branch to create a saddle position, in the middle

Chapter Four: Caring for Your New Green Tree Python

of which they rest their heads. They also have a prehensile tail which they can use to move around between the branches of trees. They will occasionally descend to the ground – usually when hunting or when moving between trees.

These are solitary creatures, and they are also nocturnal. They can strike and constrict their prey while hanging from a branch using its strong, prehensile tail. They can strike whether hanging from a tree, or even when level on the ground.

Based on these behavioral traits, the proper setup of a Green Tree Python's habitat should factor in heating, lighting, humidity, and the cage structure itself, which should be properly sized and outfitted with a suitable perch and substrate.

The Basics of Reptile Thermoregulation

Thermoregulation is the act by which an animal controls or regulates his body temperature. For warm blooded animals such as mammals and birds, this is done through a combination of internal processes and external factors. For reptiles such as snakes, however, thermoregulation is exclusively an external matter.

Chapter Four: Caring for Your New Green Tree Python

Snakes and other reptiles are classified as ectotherms, which means that they have no internal means of regulating body heat or metabolic function – as opposed to endotherms like mammals and birds that rely partly on caloric intake for energy. Snakes rely entirely on external sources for means of regulating their body temperature – either to stay warm or to keep from overheating. This is why the environment you prepare for your Green Tree Python is crucial.

There are three ways by which snakes and reptiles regulate their body temperature:

- Gaining heat via radiation, such as via sunlight
- Gaining heat via conduction, as when the ground temperature is higher than its body temperature
- Losing heat via convection, or when the air temperature is lower than its body temperature

You can observe thermoregulation activities among snakes and reptiles in the wild through various activities: they could bask in sunlight while lying on a rock, or they could seek shelter in the shade and away from direct sunlight. Essentially, they would have to move to where it is warmer or cooler, depending on what their body needs. In artificial conditions such as in an enclosure or terrarium, you will have to provide them with heat source that is variable enough within the enclosure so that they can seek a cooler spot should they need it. Among snake keepers, this is called a heat gradient.

Green Tree Python Caging

Despite being arboreal snakes, you don't really need to provide Green Tree Pythons with tall enclosures to replicate heights from a tree. Most of their movement is horizontal – across branches, not vertically up and down trees. And providing them with a too-large enclosure might actually make the snake – particularly the juvenile ones - feel anxious and stressed. A good rule of thumb is that they should be able to stretch out to at least two-thirds their length.

The good news is that there is a wide variety of snake and reptile terrariums and enclosures currently available. Some are made of plastic, others of glass, and they are properly ventilated while also outfitted with a secure lid. You might want to sit down for some time and think about what it is that you want in a cage – are you after something that is easy to clean, aesthetic display, or something else? Then consider your budget. The wide variety of snake cages available can range from less than $100 to as high as $7,000. Depending on the size and age of the snake you are aiming to get, pick your desired cage size. Having a good idea of

Chapter Four: Caring for Your New Green Tree Python

your budget, the cage size you are looking to get, and the main purpose you want the cage to serve will go a long way in helping you filter through the wide variety of snake cages available.

After you have bought your snake cage, the next step is to provision it well. You will need to provide a perch for your Green Tree Python – ideally several climbing branches of varying sizes. This would provide them with a more enriching environment and choices of movement and resting positions. Some might prefer to keep the cages clear of other decorations other than newspaper for substrate to promote greater ease in cleaning, but adding in a live plant or two will not only make the cage more beautiful to look at, it will also help promote humidity within the enclosure. It is also for this reason that some opt for substrate made of mulch or coconut husks, which can hold moisture for several days.

Finally, your python's cage should be provisioned with a water bowl. This can be used by your pet to drink water from, but because Green Tree Pythons usually just drink off the sprayed mist from their coils, the primary use of such a water bowl is to help with the humidity.

Chapter Four: Caring for Your New Green Tree Python

Heating Requirements

The environment in tropical rainforests is usually warm and humid, and the temperature rarely goes below 70 degrees Fahrenheit. To be able to replicate this in a cage means providing supplemental heating sources – either baseline or hot spot, or both. An example of the former are under tank heater, and an example of the latter are basic light bulbs, ceramic heat emitters, or heat panels.

These heat sources should be distributed around your snake cage so as to provide your Green Tree Python with a variety of temperatures within which it can move. This is called a "heat gradient." In their natural environment, they can bask in the heat during the day at temperatures of around 88 degrees, sometimes retreating to lower ambient temperatures as they seek to thermoregulate. There should be a warmer area and a cooler area within the enclosure. In no instance, however, should the temperature fall below 70-72 degrees, even at night.

Be careful when you select regular incandescent bulbs as one of your heat sources as this will also impact the lighting and day/night control cycles. You might want to pick out a ceramic heater to substitute occasionally for the bulbs, rotating them as needed, which would also keep down the risks of electrical overheating or malfunctions. If

Chapter Four: Caring for Your New Green Tree Python

you only have a small cage for a juvenile Green Tree Python, however, then an under tank heater and a ceramic heater might be sufficient.

All artificial heating sources should be kept outside of the cage so as to protect the snake from being burned. Invest in a good thermostat that would measure your temperature while also regulating the actual temperature inside the cage by automatically turning your heat source on and off as needed. You might also want to double check this manually, checking the cage with a regular thermometer to confirm the readings on your thermostat – which can certainly sometimes fail. Even with a thermostat, it is always a good idea to use a gauge.

Lighting Requirements

During a 24 hour period, snakes need at least 12 hours of light followed by 12 hours of darkness. A simple timer can help you regulate the lighting cycle.

Full spectrum lighting can be a great addition to your terrarium as it can bring out the vibrant colors of your Green Tree Python. But chondros don't really need full spectrum light to help them with synthesizing vitamins, minerals and calcium. On the other hand, you shouldn't use regular light

Chapter Four: Caring for Your New Green Tree Python

bulbs that you can buy from your hardware store, either. There are specialized lights for reptiles that you can purchase from pet stores. These are intended to provide your pet with UV light that will supply your pet with the proper amount of UVA and UVB rays that your python will use in regulating their metabolism, to synthesize vitamins and minerals, and to metabolize calcium and help keep their bones strong. These types of lightning sources are intended to mimic natural ight as much as possible.

This 12-hour cycle of light and dark is important for animals – particularly for nocturnal ones like the Green Tree Python. While you may be turning off the lights for your terrarium or snake cage for 12 hours, don't forget that room lighting can have a significant impact on your python. Once you have established your 12-12 hour cycle, try not to "shock" your pet by turning on the lights inside the room where they are kept during the 12 hours when it is supposed to be dark for them. This can lead to sleep deprivation, which can also lead to a number of other problems – whether it pertains to their health or temperament.

Be careful when choosing incandescent bulbs and the wattage they will consume. Higher wattage produces more heat, and this can significantly raise the temperatures within the enclosure.

Chapter Four: Caring for Your New Green Tree Python

Maintaining Humidity

There should be a humidity range of 40 to 70 percent within the snake cage – misting can help you promote humidity within the enclosure, but remember that it should never be constantly wet within the cage as this can lead to dermal infections in your pet. Humidity levels can rise for brief periods such as after misting, but this should be followed by dry periods in between.

This is similar to the alternating periods of rains and sunshine within a tropical jungle environment, or a "flood and dry" cycle. While you can use any type of spray bottle for the misting, adjustable cage vents can also help you dry out the environment within the cage in the interim. Basically, the cage should be thoroughly dry by the time you mist the next time. A hygrometer will help you to measure the humidity levels within the cage's environment.

Useful Tools and Devices

Now you are probably realizing why a Green Tree Python is considered an intermediate snake for keepers. The environment of their habitat alone needs on-hands maintenance and a thorough knowledge of what is needed.

Chapter Four: Caring for Your New Green Tree Python

Thankfully, there are a number of devices and gadgets that can help you monitor these various environmental factors, to make sure that your python's habitat is optimal for it to thrive and flourish. A mistake in any of these – light, heat, or humidity, can cause various problems in your pet such as illnesses or diseases, behavioral changes, and sometimes even death – such as if temperature rises too high and causes them to dry out.

Some of the tools or gadgets you may want to invest in and familiarize yourself with include:

- A simple light timer to automate the on/off cycles of your light sources
- A thermometer to help you measure the heat and temperature
- A thermostat to help you in regulating the temperature by turning heating sources on and off as needed
- A rheostat can act as a dimmer, reducing or increasing the amount of power that goes to a certain device such as a light or heat source
- A hygrometer to help you monitor the humidity levels

Chapter Five: Meeting Your Green Tree Python's Nutritional Needs

Green Tree Pythons are carnivores, and their diet in a natural environment consists mostly of small mammals such as rodents and smaller reptiles. Occasionally, juvenile snakes may also feed on small lizards and frogs. Because they eat their prey whole, this simplifies their nutritional needs quite a bit. All you need to do is supply them with enough whole rodents and a steady provision of water, and a python with a healthy appetite can thrive quite easily in captivity. Mostly, the concern in feeding snakes such as the Green Tree Python has more to do with how to feed them, how much, and how often.

Chapter Five: Meeting Your Green Tree Python's Nutritional Needs

Prey Items to Feed Green Tree Pythons

Caring for snakes such as the Green Tree Python means that you will have to deal with the fact that you will have to purchase, store, and feed rodents of various sizes to your pet. This is not a field for the squeamish. You and the rest of your family will have to accept that there will need to be frozen little mice stored in a freezer in your home. Frozen packages of dead mice and rats of various sizes or ages can usually be bought from pet supply stores. For sanitary and health reasons, you should store these separately from your own food items.

It is always a good idea to sit down with your family and discuss this with them to make sure they are all on board. This would also minimize unwanted surprises should one of your family members one day rummage through the freezer for food items.

Prey items come in various sizes: pinkies, fuzzies, hoppers, weans, smalls, and adults. The Green Tree Python is a naturally slender snake, and they have slow metabolisms so it is better to feed conservatively in terms of size. Some breeders recommend feeding them a frozen mouse that is no larger than the largest portion of your python's body. After being ingested, the swallowed prey

Chapter Five: Meeting Your Green Tree Python's Nutritional Needs

item should just be large enough that it produces a noticeable lump (never a bulge) after having been consumed. It is always better to err on the side of caution and feed them smaller food items than to feed them rodent sizes that seem too large.

A general guide to feeding schedules is set out in the table below:

Stage	Frequency
Hatchlings	Every 5-7 days
Juveniles	Twice a week
Adults	Every 7 to 14 days

A hatchling will start out with newborn pinkies, and the size of the prey item will increase as your python grows.

While using a separate feeding enclosure may not always be necessary, some owners do prefer to feed their pythons in separate enclosures from their primary habitat to ensure greater ease in cleaning. If you are keeping more than one snake, a separate housing for feeding may prove to be necessary.

Chapter Five: Meeting Your Green Tree Python's Nutritional Needs

Feeding Fresh vs. Killed Prey

There are some keepers that prefer feeding fresh or live prey to their snakes because it emulates natural conditions for their pythons more closely than feeding only killed or dead prey. The claim is that predatory pythons such as the Green Tree species need to develop their instincts and skills, and they also need the thrill of hunting and catching live prey. This provides them with mental and physical stimulation that they simply will not get from a steady diet of killed food items. Such exertions will also provide them with enough exercise to reduce the chances of overfeeding and/or obesity.

But feeding live prey to a Green Tree Python does have its risks. Live rats and rodents, for instance, can actually harm, injure, or even kill your snake. If you do decide to feed live prey to your snake, close supervision is always advised. If your python has not hunted and/or killed or attacked the live prey in its enclosure within a few hours, it is better to remove the live prey lest it attack your snake.

The other alternative is feeding killed prey – and this is the more popular choice among snake keepers. This completely eliminates the dangers of injury, scarring or death that your snake may get from being fed live prey.

Chapter Five: Meeting Your Green Tree Python's Nutritional Needs

Those who advocate the feeding of killed prey also claim that Green Tree Pythons don't really need the thrill of the hunt. Sufficient mental and physical stimulation can be derived from the overall environment that you create for your pet.

Whether you choose to feed your python live or killed prey, each alternative requires the taking of certain precautions. Live prey should be provided with their own food source so that they do not attack your python. Should an attack happen, bring your pet to a veterinarian immediately.

On the other hand, the feeding of killed prey can often require hands-on assistance, patience and persistence on your part. Tongs are used to dangle the prey item near the Green Tree Python. Some might attack immediately and go after the food, but if they don't, you will have to entice the snake to feed. You can do this by:

- "walking" the prey as though it were still alive,
- rubbing it against your snake
- warming it until it has temperatures that are higher than room temperature
- make the prey item smell better by dipping it in a dish of warm chicken broth or piercing the prey's braincase with a pin to release more enticing odors.

Chapter Five: Meeting Your Green Tree Python's Nutritional Needs

Tips for Feeding Your Green Tree Python

- Feeding frozen/thawed prey items reduces the chances of diseases and parasites in the snakes, and reduces the chances of injury
- Pre-killed prey can be stored in a freezer for up to six months.
- Before feeding, pre-killed prey should be thawed completely and warmed to slightly above room temperature. This is because Green Tree Pythons hunt using heat pits.
- Never use your fingers to dangle food in front of your pet. Use tongs, tweezers or a hemostat to handle prey items instead. This reduces your risks of snake bites as a ravenous snake can strike at anything that moves, and that includes your fingers.
- If your snake is not used to feeding on killed prey items, and you have decided not to feed them live prey, the habit of eating killed prey can easily be developed. Use the tips above that would make the prey more enticing for your pet. Remember to practice both patience and persistence as you train your python to feed on killed prey items. It can be challenging and even frustrating, but also rewarding

Chapter Five: Meeting Your Green Tree Python's Nutritional Needs

and, in terms of long term care and feeding of your pet – will ultimately prove worthwhile
- On the other hand, don't overfeed your pet, either. Overfeeding will not only result in obesity, but in some animals this can also cause prolapse
- Use slow, deliberate movements when you are feeding your snake. Snakes can react aggressively to sudden movements – either as a defense mechanism or because of its predatory instinct. Once you have successfully fed your python, and the snake has the foot clamped firmly in its strong jaws, don't make any sudden or jerky movements. Allow it sufficient quiet and undisturbed time to finish swallowing the entire meal.
- Fresh water should be available to your pet at all times. Snakes will use readily available water to either drink from, or to soak in, so the bowl has to be large enough to accommodate your pet, allowing it to fully submerge. This will help the snake when it comes time for them to shed. Clean and refill the water bowl at least twice a week.

Chapter Five: Meeting Your Green Tree Python's Nutritional Needs

Possible Feeding Problems

A healthy snake should have a healthy appetite, and will eat regularly. But what if they refuse to eat? As long as they are eating, you can be reasonably certain that they are getting sufficient nutrients from their food. A few other possible feeding problems include:

- Refusal of a meal several times in a row
- If your snake regurgitates its meal
- Obvious weight loss
- Signs of disease such as fluid or bubbles in the nostrils, sneezing, or open-mouthed breathing.

Don't force feed your Green Tree Python just to get him to eat – especially if you do not have experience. Force feeding requires handling the snake while you force food down its throat using tongs or tweezers. If you aren't sure about what you're doing, you can really injure the snake – whether in your handling of them, or in how you feed them. Best to take them to a veterinarian first so that you can identify the cause of your pet's feeding problems.

Chapter Six: Green Tree Python Husbandry

Husbandry is the term used by snake keepers to refer to the regular and daily care of your pet snake. Two of the most important facets of snake husbandry have already been discussed in the previous chapters: housing and feeding. In this chapter, we take a look at some of the other aspects types of husbandry care and maintenance that you will need to do to make sure that your Green Tree Python is kept clean, safe, and in good health.

Cleaning and Disinfecting the Snake Cage and Habitat

Chapter Six: Green Tree Python Husbandry

Aside from providing appropriate heating, lighting, humidity, and cage structures and décor, you will also want to clean your Green Tree Python's care regularly. This is particularly important as the prevailing humidity within the enclosure can be a perfect ground for the growth of bacteria. Most reptiles can be prone to skin and bacterial infection if left alone in unclean surroundings for long.

You will need to make a habit of routine cage maintenance and cleaning. Not only will this keep the interior of the enclosure clean, odor-free and healthy, but it also keeps you and your family safe and healthy. Regular cleaning prevents the possible transmission of diseases like Salmonella, which can be found in the fecal matter of reptiles, and which may be transmissible to humans.

Spot cleaning the interior of the cage should be done as often as possible – at least once a day, or once every other day. Spot cleaning your reptile's cage can include:

- The removal of fecal matter as soon as you notice them.
- The removal of shed skin
- The removal of uneaten food
- Cleaning and refilling the water bowls at least twice a week.

A more thorough cage cleaning should be done at least once a month, ideally more. During this process, you

Chapter Six: Green Tree Python Husbandry

will need to relocate the snake so that you can clean and sterilize the entire cage components, including perches, decorations, substrate, etc. To be able to do this thoroughly, you will need to temporarily relocate your python to a different holding cage or cell. As usual, make sure that this cage is secure and clean, and is sufficiently ventilated.

Begin by removing all of the cage items, disposing directly of the substrate which you will be replacing completely. Set aside these cage items in a bowl or container. You will now proceed to clean the inside of the terrarium or cage, and then later on to disinfect and sterilize the cage items. Gather the following materials to help you in your cleaning tasks:

- A spray bottle
- Brushes, q-tips, putty knives, or razor blades
- Buckets
- Terrarium cleaner that is safe for reptiles
- Paper towels
- Robber gloves
- Sponges

Make sure that all the electrical components of the cage – such as heating and lighting, are turned off or unplugged. Then armed with a spray bottle, a sponge, gloves, and just regular soap and water, begin to clean the interior of the snake cage as thoroughly as possible. Make use of instruments such as brushes, q-tips, putty knives, or razor blades to really get at the hardened feces or waste that a regular paper towel won't be able to dislodge. Really get into it, using herp-safe terrarium cleaners for the really troublesome spots and corners. Rinse the inside of the cage thoroughly.

Clean and disinfect the cage items by boiling them in water for some 30 minutes. Try to avoid using regular household chemical cleaners which may prove toxic or harmful to your pet. Besides, even using these types of cleansers cannot really guarantee the thorough elimination of bacteria. The only way to be sure is to kill any thriving bacteria through high heat and boiling temperatures as you thoroughly sterilize each cage item.

Use a disinfectant to give another through cleaning to all the cage items, including the interior of the snake cage. Then use hot water to rinse of all chemical residue. Allow it all to air-dry, making sure that the cage interior and all the various cage items and implements are thoroughly dried.

When you're done, reinstall all the cage items and decorations, this time putting on a new layer of fresh substrate. You might also want to give your Green Tree Python a bath before allowing it to return to its newly cleaned and dry terrarium.

Chapter Six: Green Tree Python Husbandry

Wash and disinfect all your cleaning tools and equipment with the same thoroughness that you practiced when you were cleaning the cage interior and the cage items. And finally, wash your hands thoroughly – using hot, soapy water. Don't forget to finish off with a disinfectant, too.

Tips for Bathing a Green Tree Python

Bathing a pet snake is a simple and straightforward process – but with loads of benefits for your pet. Bathing can help relieve constipation in your snake, and it can also kill mites and promotes shedding. An occasional bath for your Green Tree Python can therefore go a long way to having a happy and healthy snake.

Use warm spring or filtered water. Don't use tap or chlorinated water as the chemicals in the water can actually irritate their skin. And because they are sensitive to temperature changes, you'll want to provide them with a reasonably warm bath. A good range between 100 and 105 degrees Fahrenheit is a good level for a snake bath.

Because you don't want your Green Tree Python getting away from you during bathing time, you might want to place a sufficiently roomy bowl of the warm bath water in

Chapter Six: Green Tree Python Husbandry

an enclosure. You can help your snake get into the bath, but more often than not, they will quickly bathe themselves.

Just let him swim freely around in the water for around 10 to 15 minutes. When he is done, pick him up, gently use a towel to dry him off, and then return him to his now clean, sterilized, disinfected, and thoroughly dried habitat. Some recommend placing your snake in a holding cage immediately after a bath as some snakes can defecate immediately after a bath, and you don't want him doing this too soon within the newly cleaned cage. Give your python sufficient time in the holding cage to do his business before moving him back to his home.

Chapter Seven: Green Tree Python Handling and Temperament

Green Tree Pythons may have a reputation for being an aggressive species, but this is usually dependent on individual snakes. A snake bred in captivity under optimal conditions will certainly not be as aggressive as a Green Tree Python that was captured from the wild, and then later underwent the stresses of being shipped across long distances. Your best bet when looking for a Green Tree Python pet is to find one that was bred in captivity, preferably from a reputable breeder near your location so that the stresses of transportation, shipping and acclimatization are kept to a minimum. Besides which, a

Chapter Seven: Green Tree Python Handling and Temperament

snake born and bred by humans is far more likely to be docile and familiar with humans and with an environment of captivity.

That said, this is still a potentially dangerous creature, and you should always keep this in mind whenever you handle your Green Tree Python. No matter how docile they may seem at any given moment, this is a species that will never be completely tamed.

Green Tree Python Temperament

Green Tree Pythons can be a feisty species to handle, but once habituated to occasional human contact, they can be handled if done with care. The reputation for ill-tempered Green Tree Pythons that bite are more often the result of bad handling.

But this species of snake is really more for display than handling. Spending time with your pet snake will eventually lead them to tolerate the occasional handling, but they will never truly become fond of it. Occasional, stress-free handling for brief periods of time can be done, provided you do it right. If what you are looking for is a pet with which you can socialize on a regular basis, then this is probably not the right pet for you.

Chapter Seven: Green Tree Python Handling and Temperament

Green Tree Pythons don't like being taken out of their cage, nor do they like a foreign "invasion" of their area. When stressed in this way, they can possibly turn aggressive. If they have a history of being grabbed, physically restrained, or handled and treated roughly, they might display a defensive and aggressive front when approached.

Tips for Handling Your Green Tree Python

Below are some tips and guidelines to keep in mind as you handle your Green Tree Python pet. Remember always to keep calm and to make your actions slow and deliberate. Pay attention to the snake's responses - often enough, your pet's reaction will vary – based on the stress they may feel or how you approach them. Other influencing factors could be individual and varying temperaments between individual snakes – not all will react the same way, and this is mostly due to their individual experiences of being handled.

Once you do manage to lift your Green Tree Python out of its cage and be able to handle it in your hands and arms, keep your movements slow, deliberate, and moderate. Keep these handling sessions brief, because the longer they

Chapter Seven: Green Tree Python Handling and Temperament

are kept outside of the comfort of their cage, the more stressed they will become. Again, always remember to approach them with respect – this can be a dangerous pet if approached wrongly and without due regard to the dangers they can pose to you or to the people around you.

- Avoid handling or approaching your Green Tree Python at night (or during the 12-hour darkness cycle in their cage). These are nocturnal animals, and their instincts are usually on high alert during this time – whether to hunt prey or to defend their territory. They can respond instinctively to any form of movement during this time, so putting a hand inside its cage could simply be an invitation for it to bite you.
- Avoid handling young Green Tree Pythons which are under a year old. At this age, they are still extremely delicate and can easily be damaged by inappropriate handling. Wait until they have grown and matured a bit, and their bodies have become less delicate and able to withstand the stress of being physically handled.
- Use slow, deliberate movements when approaching or handling your Green Tree Python. Don't make any sudden movements, as your pet can interpret this as

Chapter Seven: Green Tree Python Handling and Temperament

either a prey to hunt, or an enemy to defend against. Pay attention to how they respond to your movements. If they seem to respond actively, going on high alert, this is probably not the best time to approach them. On the other hand, if they remain restful and relaxed, chances are good that they will not resist or fight against human handling. Remain calm and deliberate in your movements throughout.

- Probably the best way to handle a Green Tree Python is to lift their perch straight out of their cage instead of seeking to separate them from their perch. Support them from beneath – never from approach them from the top, which they can view as threatening. Support the snake's lower coils, and as you lift them or raise their coils, wait for them to voluntarily disentangle their tails from their perch. Never pull or force them to let go of their perch. Doing so may actually damage their vertebra and cause spinal aberrations.

Behavioral Characteristics of the Green Tree Pythons

This section contains a general guideline on the behavioral characteristics of the Green Tree Python – each of which should be useful during the handling and husbandry of these snakes. Although chondros will have unique and

Chapter Seven: Green Tree Python Handling and Temperament

individual character traits that the keeper will become familiar with after years of familiarity, there are common behaviors among all Green Tree Pythons that can be used as guide in reading the python's activities and conduct.

- Pythons generally do not attack humans unless startled or provoked, so you should use slow and deliberate movements. Brooding females can be aggressive as they act to protect their eggs.
- These are ambush predators, which means that they will remain motionless in a camouflaged ambush position before striking suddenly at passing prey. In the wilds, a Green Tree Python will hold onto a branch with the use of its prehensile tail, and strike out at a prey from an s-shaped position. The color stages that the Green Tree Python goes through throughout its life cycle is also utilized to promote camouflage - the red or yellow colors of young snakes blend better in forest gaps or edges where the smaller prey reside, while the adult green coloration is best in the closed canopy of the forest, where larger prey can be found.
- Green Tree Pythons are constrictors – using their sharp, backward-curving teeth, they will grasp the prey to restrain it, and then wrap it around with coils. They do not usually crush their prey to death, as

Chapter Seven: Green Tree Python Handling and Temperament

opposed to contrary beliefs. Death results primarily from asphyxiation, as the prey is unable to move its ribs to breathe while it is being constricted.

- This is primarily an arboreal species, which means that they spend most of their time in trees or low shrubs. They are also nocturnal, with periods of resting and sleep primarily during the daytime.
- The juveniles of this species will spend most of their time near the ground, in the shadows and where their bright red shading or yellow coloring will blend well with leaves and other debris of the forest floor. It is only when they begin to mature and take on adult green coloration do they begin to move higher into the tree canopies. This process of color changing is known as ontogenesis, and occurs between 1 to 4 years of age.
- Pythons have infrared-sensitive receptors in deep grooves in their snout, which allows them to "see" the radiated heat of warm-blooded prey. They use their forked tongues to both "smell" and taste – thus allowing them to track their prey – the tongues collect airborne particles which are passed on to the Jacobson's organ in the mouth for examination. They can also perceive movement through their undersides, which are sensitive to vibrations in the ground.

Chapter Seven: Green Tree Python Handling and Temperament

- Snakes have specialized belly scales which can grip surfaces and which they use to travel or climb. Snake scales are extensions of their epidermis – so shedding removes the complete outer layer as a single unit, rather than separately. This is called shedding, molting, or sloughing, and is useful in replacing old and worn skin while also getting rid of external parasites such as mites and ticks.
- Prior to shedding, the snake stops eating and retreats or hides in a safe place. Their skin becomes dull and dry looking, and their eyes turn cloudy or blue-colored. The inner surface of the skin liquefies at this point, which separates the old skin from the new skin. When the snake is ready – typically after a few days – the eyes clear again and the snake crawls out of its old skin. Akin to a sock being turned inside out, the old skin breaks near the mouth, and through wriggling and rubbing against rough surfaces, the snake comes out of its old skin – which is peeled back over the body in one piece, from head to tail. The new skin is typically larger and brighter than the old one.
- While adult snakes may shed its skin only once or twice a year, younger or juvenile and growing snakes can shed up to four times a year.

Chapter Eight: Breeding Your Green Tree Python

Many of the Green Tree Pythons now being kept as pets by private owners were the result of captive breeding processes. Many people now are breeding Green Tree Pythons – in Indonesia, this species have been bred in captivity for years. We have already learned much about best practices in breeding this python, and while many of the challenges have been overcome, this is still not an easy species to breed.

The truth is that while breeders may have successfully promoted captive breeding, we still do not

Chapter Eight: Breeding Your Green Tree Python

know much about this species' breeding practices in the wild. The actual mating season is not known, and it does not seem as though breeding takes place every year. Much of the information that we do have about the Green Tree Python's breeding and reproduction processes come from the many breeders who have successfully bred Green Tree Pythons in captivity.

Sexing

A successful breeding program begins with a healthy breeding pair. Females usually reach sexual maturity after 3.6 years, while the sexual maturity of males occurs after 2.4 years. And the process by which you can identify whether a snake is a male or a female is called sexing.

Sexing can be done in either one of two ways: by popping or probing. Please take note that you should never sex hatchlings. They are very sensitive and delicate at this stage, and attempting to sex them can injure them severely. It is recommended that sexing be done only after a Green Tree Python is at least a year old, and weighs more than 100 grams.

Popping is done by applying pressure with the thumb just below the vent. This will cause the hemipenes of a male to evert.

Probing – which is the more commonly employed means of sexing – is done by gently inserting a lubricated

Chapter Eight: Breeding Your Green Tree Python

probe into the side of the vent, and then sliding them into the pockets that are found on either side of the tail. For males, the probe will slide to a depth of approximately 10 scales, while for a female, it will go for only 3 or 4 scales. Sometimes the probe will only go somewhere between these two ranges, and these are often classified as unsexed snakes. Probing isn't always definitive or certain, and other factors may influence the result such as the pressure you exert on the probe, or something blocking the pockets so you could not insert the probe deep enough. It is essential that you don't try to attempt to probe your snake if you do not have sufficient experience with sexing. A mistake here can injure and damage your snake, and there is always the chance that the results of your probe can be wrong.

More often than not, a determination of a snake's sex can be established from their behavior. Males are generally more active than females. They also tend to refuse food during breeding time. But perhaps the best sign that your snake is a male is when he everts his hemipenes when he is defecating. When he sheds his skin, the hemipenes can be identified as two dried bits of skin at the vent – but which should not be confused with a small bump that can also show in the shed skin of females. Their tail shape can also differ, with the male's being more parallel and bulbous, as opposed to the female's tail which is more tapered in shape.

Chapter Eight: Breeding Your Green Tree Python

For a breeding pair, females should ideally be bigger and weightier than males. This is to allow them to have sufficient body weight that can undergo the stress of egg production. Females are usually paired only after they have reached 750 to 800 grams, which they can reach around the age of 3 or 4 years. Males, on the other hand, have been bred successfully at a weight of only 270 grams, usually at around 2 ½ to 3 years old. The selected breeding pair must both be in good health, with good body weight and muscle tone.

Thermal Cycling and Cooling

Green Tree Pythons are seasonal breeders. In the wild, breeding seems to be stimulated by low pressure fronts and storms. In captivity, the same results can be stimulated by dropping the cage temperatures gradually over a period of time. A gradual decrease in the nighttime temperatures until it reaches the low 70 degrees Fahrenheit range, and a more moderate decrease of about 2 to 4 degrees in the daytime temperature, over a period of a few weeks, would work to trigger reproductive interest in both the male and the female. In a way, this is a signal to them that the summer season is changing over into the cooler periods of the year.

Chapter Eight: Breeding Your Green Tree Python

The length of daylight may also impact the breeding cycle in Green Tree Pythons. In the wild, the days do begin to shorten as winter approaches – and this is replicated in artificial conditions by gradually working the daytime heating periods from 12 to 8 or 7 hours. Sometimes, you can simply mimic what happens outdoors, with the drops in temperature starting around August until January.

There are no hard and fast rules as to how long you should promote thermal cycling. Some breeders do this for around 3 or 4 weeks before finally placing the male with the female python. You will usually observe the male pacing his cage at this time – this means that he is now actively looking for a female.

Introduction and Mating

Receptive pairs will usually mate within hours after being put together. This happens by the male crawling over the female and spurring her with his spurs. The mating itself usually begins in the evening, and it can last for a few hours to sometimes an entire day, though typically it finishes in the morning.

The period of breeding or copulation should last for several weeks, though it may sometimes happen that the

Chapter Eight: Breeding Your Green Tree Python

males lose interest in the female after some time. If this happens, ways of eliciting mating include taking out the male for a few days and then reintroducing them again. Spraying or misting can also work to promote mating.

After breeding together or copulating for several weeks, you may notice changes in the female which can include a loss of interest in food, and a color change wherein her overall color may grow dull. Some may even take on a predominantly blue coloration. Internally, the female will begin to swell with developing egg follicles, and the male will naturally lose interest in her at this time.

Ovulation and Pre-Lay Shed

Signs that the female has begun ovulating include a large, mid-body swelling as though she had just eaten a very large meal. This swelling typically lasts from 12 to 24 hours. She may also appear uncomfortable and restless. Watch out for her next shed after this, which can happen approximately 29 days after ovulation. This is called a pre-lay shed, and will normally take longer than a normal shed. You can probably expect the eggs to be deposited after 14 to 21 days, or some two to three weeks after the pre-lay shed.

Chapter Eight: Breeding Your Green Tree Python

Laying Eggs

The gestation period for a gravid female Green Tree Python is approximately 50 days after ovulation, or around 21 days after the pre-lay shed. Around the 40th day, or around a week before she is ready to lay her eggs, she will pass any remaining fecal matter in her system, and will begin looking for a suitable place to lay her eggs.

A nesting box should be provided for her in the cage – and this can be constructed of either wood or plastic, with a lid and an entrance hole large enough to accommodate the passage of two coils of her body at the same time. Some can use an improvised box, lidded plastic buckets, ice cream containers, or even overturned flower pots. A good size for the nesting box would be around 8 inches by 8 inches wide by 12 inches high. Lining should be provided at the bottom of the nesting box to prevent the eggs from sticking to the box itself. Some make good use of dry sphagnum moss, newspaper, coconut fiber, or vermiculite.

Be careful where you place the box in the cage – make sure that it is not directly connected or near a light and heat source, or you risk overheating the eggs.

Sometimes, the female will refuse to use the nesting box you have provided for her. Some might lay the eggs directly while they are on the perch – so you need to provide a thick enough lining at the bottom of the cage to help cushion the eggs as they fall. Others might even choose to lay their eggs in the water bowl. To prevent the eggs from drowning, you might want to reduce the water content in the bowl to at least a centimeter or so when the time is nearing for the female to lay her eggs. There are even breeders who remove the water bowls and perches from within the cage altogether in preparation for the arrival of the eggs.

Brooding or Incubation

The average clutch size of a Green Tree Python is around 12 to 18 eggs, though sometimes this can reach as high as 40 or more eggs. In the wild, the female broods over the eggs for a period of about 50 days more or less, during which she will refuse to eat until the eggs are hatched. For this reason, many breeders prefer artificial incubation to allow the female a faster recovery. Females typically refuse eating from the period of ovulation until hatching, and coupled with the physical demand of having produced and laid the eggs, the female's physical condition is at risk of deteriorating quite rapidly. A significant amount of weight loss is to be expected – which makes her recovery that much harder.

Chapter Eight: Breeding Your Green Tree Python

Opting for maternal incubation also makes it more difficult for you to check on the eggs. A single bad egg can cause the entire clutch to deteriorate, so some form of monitoring or examination of the eggs is important – something that would be difficult to do in cases of maternal incubation.

For all these reasons, artificial incubation is often considered the more feasible option. Fortunately, there are high quality incubators readily available in the market for reasonable prices. Other breeders opt to build their own.

You need to remove the female from the eggs around which she would have coiled. Simply lift her coils until she is removed from the eggs. Many times this can be done without any fuss, but if you are dealing with a more aggressive female, you might need more than one person to help accomplish this – one to hold the female's head, and the other to lift her coils.

The eggs will often be stuck together in a clump. Separate them carefully to place them in individual trays to prevent bad or rotting eggs from contaminating the rest. Be careful as you do this so you do not tear the eggs, though a small tear is not necessarily fatal, and the egg can still go to full term to hatch.

Traditionally, incubation media of sphagnum moss, vermiculite and perlite were used with great success. More

Chapter Eight: Breeding Your Green Tree Python

recently, however, most breeders have shifted to a no-substrate method of incubation where the eggs are suspended on a rack above a reservoir of water. This allows the incubation container to maintain steady levels of humidity without the egg coming into contact with moist or wet substrate media. This container is largely sealed, with only very small holes for ventilation. Occasionally, you should open the container to promote air exchange – at least once a week at first, then at least daily within the final week near hatching. Make sure that no condensation forms on the lid of the container which can cause moisture to drip down onto the eggs as this can cause the eggs to spoil. As much as possible, the eggs should not come into contact with or be exposed to wet or moist surfaces.

The incubation container should be maintained at temperatures of approximately 87 to 88 degrees - any higher than 90 degrees can be lethal for the eggs. Humidity levels should also be maintained at above 90 percent throughout the incubation period, which lasts for around 50 days, after which the eggs are ready to hatch.

Hatching

Towards the time near hatching, replace the water at the bottom of the container with damp paper towels to

Chapter Eight: Breeding Your Green Tree Python

prevent the drowning of any hatchlings that may emerge. You may also wish to provide a perch or two to provide them a place to rest after they have emerged from the egg.

The neonate or hatchling will first poke its head out after the egg is slit, and it will sit like this for some time – usually between 12 to 48 hours. Don't try to pull the hatchling out, or to help them out of the egg if this happens – they may still be absorbing some of the yolk from inside the egg. But if the egg begins to degrade and the neonate still refuses to leave, some gentle prodding will encourage it to finally move and exit from the egg.

At hatching, neonate green tree pythons measure approximately 30.5 cm in length and weigh in at an average of 8-15 grams. Their color will either be brick-red or bright yellow. Each of them should be set up in individual plastic tubs where they should be kept well-hydrated until they shed – some 10 days after hatching. Provide them with a simple perch, a water bowl, and a heat source.

Feeding should be initiated by tease-feeding the neonates with pre-killed or frozen/thawed pinkies that are no larger than the snake's diameter at mid-body. Some might initially be shy or retiring and patience is required to get them to feed successfully. Once they catch on, however, they can feed quite eagerly. Feeding can be done approximately 5-7 days after the first meals were accepted.

Chapter Eight: Breeding Your Green Tree Python

Chapter Nine: Keeping Your Green Tree Python Healthy

With the provision of a well-equipped, well-designed cage that can maintain the correct necessary environment for the Green Tree Python, most of the rest of this species' husbandry is pretty straightforward. Feed them well, keep their area clean and sanitized as much as possible, and chances are that your pet snake will thrive for many long years.

Most of the health issues that can crop up in Green Tree Pythons usually result from major deviations in their environmental requirements, which is why a good enclosure or cage is essential. The two most common health issues

Chapter Nine: Keeping Your Green Tree Python Healthy

they can suffer from include respiratory infections and rectal prolapsed.

Green Tree Pythons can still be prone to various other health conditions, which are discussed in this chapter, as well as information regarding available treatments, management, or prevention if any are available.

You should devote some time to locating a good veterinarian who has experience in dealing with reptiles and snakes – before you even bring your pet home. Rather unfortunately, not all vets have experience in working with reptiles, so this may also limit their working knowledge of health problems common to snakes. Finding a reliable vet in your area is a great advantage – some breeders and snake keepers actually have to drive long distances whenever they need to bring their pets to a medical professional.

Some of the various health conditions to which Green Tree Pythons are prone to include:

- Respiratory Infections
- Rectal Prolapse
- Spinal Kinks
- Tail-hanging
- Necrotic Stomatitis
- Parasites
- Water Blisters

Chapter Nine: Keeping Your Green Tree Python Healthy

Respiratory Infections

Respiratory Infections have been found to be quite common among Green Tree Pythons. Most are caused by bacteria or viruses associated with cold weather. During these times, a snake's metabolism and natural resistance is lowered. There are occasions, however, when this condition can develop even under ideal environmental conditions.

Symptoms include coughing, perching with its head tilted back, and a raspy, mucous sound during inhalation. There may also be some liquid discharge from the mouth or nostrils. Your snake will also likely be quite lethargic and lacking in appetite. Open mount breathing could indicate a significant problem.

Avoid drafts, improper temperatures and stress for your snake when this happens. Some opt to quarantine the sick snake and keep them within higher than normal temperatures, while prescribed antibiotics may be administered to address bacterial infection. A quarantine for the sick snake is important – especially if you have other pet snakes. Respiratory infections can be quite contagious and highly infectious, and it may pass on to other snakes in your collection.

Chapter Nine: Keeping Your Green Tree Python Healthy

Rectal Prolapse

Rectal Prolapse takes place when the bowel protrudes outside of the cloaca during defecation, whereby the snake subsequently is unable to retract it. It can be frightening when this happens, but usually looks much worse than it actually is. Some point to inappropriate diet as the cause, though other contributing factors may also be obesity, stress, and lack of muscle tone. A lack of exercise and dehydration may also lead to rectal prolapse.

Keep your snake well hydrated through their food, available fresh water, and humid conditions within the tank. This is also why it is important to have a good, sizeable enclosure for your Green Tree Python, with various perches to choose from. This encourages exercise and movement that can prevent this condition from developing in the first place. There are some keepers who actually take their snakes out for a "walk" out on the lawn to introduce movement and exercise.

Bring your snake to a vet for proper treatment of rectal prolapsed. This consists of moistening the swollen tissue and reinserting it back into place. Sometimes a form of adhesive material that can later be easily pulled off, such as band aid, is used around the cloaca to prevent a reoccurrence of the prolapsed. This should be followed by

Chapter Nine: Keeping Your Green Tree Python Healthy

withholding food for about two weeks, followed by controlled feeding of small prey until bowel movement normalizes.

Spinal Kinks

Spinal kinks seem to be quite prevalent among Green Tree Pythons, though most other snake species may also be affected. Spinal kinks are abnormalities in the spinal structure and the causes are as varied as genetics, physical injuries, incubation issues, or even nutrition such as insufficient calcium in their diet.

There is no effective treatment for this condition, and many times, even the specific causes are unknown. While spinal kinks can grow more pronounced as the snake matures, a snake with a kink or two in its spine can still live a long and full life. Such snakes should not be bred from, however – not only because of possible genetic factors that may influence this condition, but because of the obvious difficulty it would give to a female in ovulating and laying its eggs.

Chapter Nine: Keeping Your Green Tree Python Healthy

Tail-hanging

This is akin to constipation among snakes, and is often related to or eventually causes rectal prolapse. When fecal matter accumulates, sometimes becoming very dry, it is no longer comfortable for the snake to wrap it around its perch, and is often simply left to hang suspended from its perch.

The effort to expel the accumulated feces is certainly greater, and the difficulty of doing so may lead to the rectal prolapsed where part of the bowel extrudes when they defecate, with the snake unable to retract it. Treatment thus proceeds as for rectal prolapsed in the section above.

As with most of the other conditions that can afflict snakes, this can possibly be prevented by integrating regular schedules and lifestyle routines that promote movement, exercise, and hydration in your pet snake. Some form of exercise would help build your snake's muscle tone, as well as promote healthier digestive processes.

Chapter Nine: Keeping Your Green Tree Python Healthy

Necrotic Stomatitis

This is more commonly known as mouth canker or mouth rot, and it is a bacterial infection in the mouth that is usually caused by trauma of some sort – when the snake's mouth hits against or is exposed to a hard or rough surface. The resulting trauma can cause an injury which, if unchecked, can lead to necrotic stomatitis.

Symptoms include loss of appetite, swollen lips, and the appearance of a cheese-like substance. Bring your snake to a veterinarian if this happens. Treatment often includes the removal of the buildup, cleaning and disinfecting, and a prescribed course of antibiotics.

Parasites

Green Tree Pythons, as with most snakes, can be prone to external parasites such as mites. While not often visible to the naked eye, they can be identified by their droppings which will often make your snake look like it has been dusted with flour.

Parasites such as these are often found externally – called ectoparasites, they feed on snakes by sucking their blood.

Chapter Nine: Keeping Your Green Tree Python Healthy

There are commercially available products that work to treat mite infestations. Coupled with such treatments, one must also promote a healthy and sanitary snake enclosure that is cleaned regularly. New snakes should also be quarantined so as to prevent the passing on of potential parasites to other snakes.

Water Blisters

Water blisters are caused by excessive humidity and moisture in your snake's environment, coupled with poor ventilation. These blisters can appear as translucent, large bumps on the snake's skin that is soft to the touch. These are usually filled with fluid, but they must never be pierced. While not presenting any immediate danger to your snake's health, they can affect the next shedding when intentionally or unintentionally pierced before your snake's next molting. The effect is that the old skin may stick to the new skin, and the shedding becomes more difficult. Left alone, however, these blisters usually disappear along with the old skin.

Green Tree Python Care Sheet

This section provides a brief summary of much of the information contained in this book, and serves a ready-reference guide for those who are in a hurry to search for specific information. The most salient facts and information regarding the Green Tree Python are provided below, giving you a brief yet comprehensive overview of this magnificent and beautiful snake species, as well as what it means to own one as a pet.

1.) Basic Green Tree Python Information

Kingdom: Animalia

Phylum: Chordata

Subphylum: Vertebrata

Class: Reptilia

Order: Squamata

Suborder: Serpentes

Family: Pythonidae

Genus: Morelia

Species: Morelia Viridis

Other Names: Morelia Viridis, Python viridis, Chondropython azureus, Chondropython pulcher, Chondropython viridis

Common Names: Green Tree Python, Chondro

Regions of Origin: Indonesia (Misool, Salawati, Aru Islands, Schouten Islands, and most of Western New Guinea), Papua New Guinea (Normanby Island, the d'Entrecasteaux Islands, and nearby island with a sea level of 1,800 m elevation), Australia (Queensland and Cape York Peninsula). In Florida, USA, it is considered an invasive species.

Primary Habitat: Rainforest areas

Description: A relatively slim body, a prehensile tail, and a large and clearly defined head. The snout is large and angular.

Length: 150-180 cm (4.9-59 ft) to 200 cm (6.6 ft)

Weight: 1,100 – 1,600 g (2.4 – 3.5 lb)

Color: Juveniles start out as yellow, red, or dark brow-black. Adult colors are primarily bright green, though some retain their bright yellow juvenile colors, while others turn blue. Breeding attempts have also resulted in a host of designer colors such as tricolors, high yellow, calicos, melanistic, true blue, and super blue. A recessive morph may also result in an albino.

Conservation Status: Classified by the IUCN as "Least Concern," but is included in Appendix II of CITES (Convention on International Trade in Endangered Species of Wild Fauna and Flora), where international trade is monitored and regulated.

Primary Behavioral Characteristics: Solitary, arboreal, nocturnal, and predatory constrictor

Health Conditions: Respiratory Infections, Rectal Prolapse, Spinal Kinks, Tail-hanging, Necrotic Stomatitis, Parasites, Water Blisters

Lifespan: average 20 to 35 years

2.) Habitat Requirements

Recommended Equipment: terrarium or snake cage/enclosure, a variety of perches, water bowl, substrate, live plants, heat and light sources, thermometer, thermostat, light timer, rheostat, hygrometer

Recommended Day/Light Cycle: 12-12 hours

Recommended Temperature: 86-88 degrees Fahrenheit

Recommended Humidity Levels: 40-70 percent

Cleaning Frequency: Spot cleaning daily, with a more thorough cleaning at least 1-2 times a month

3.) Nutritional Needs

Primary Diet: Small mammals such as rodents. Juveniles may also feed on small reptiles.

Feeding Frequency (Hatchlings): every 5-7 days

Feeding Frequency (Juvenile): twice a week

Feeding Frequency (Adult): every 7-14 days

Water: Clean water in a bowl should be freely available

4.) Breeding Information

Age of Sexual Maturity (Females): 3 ½ years

Age of Sexual Maturity (Males): 2 ½ to 3 years

Thermal Cycling: lower 70 degrees Fahrenheit at nighttime, and daytime temperatures dropped by 2-3 degrees

Copulation: 4-6 weeks

Gestation Period: approximately 50 days

Ovulation: Mid-body swelling that lasts from 12 to 48 hours. This is followed by a pre-lay shed approximately 29 days later.

Egg Laying: Approximately 21 days after the pre-lay shed, 50 days after ovulation

Clutch Size: 12-30 eggs

Incubation: Approximately 50 days

Recommended Incubation Temperatures: 87-88 degrees

Recommended Incubation Humidity Levels: Above 90 percent

Length at Birth: Approximately 30.5 cm

Weight at Birth: 8-15 grams

Index

A

Acclimation	3
Active range	3
Age of Sexual Maturity	95
aggressive	68
Ambient temperature	3
anal plate	3
Annual Costs	25
Arboreal	4, 69

B

bathing	61
Behavioral Characteristics	6, 40, 67
breeders	31, 33
breeding	6, 71, 75, 95
Brooding or Incubation	7, 78
Brumation	4

C

CB	4
CH	4
Cleaning and Disinfecting the Snake Cage and Habitat	6, 57
Cleaning Frequency	94
Cloaca	4
Clutch	5, 95
Common Names	13, 92
conservation status	14, 93
Constriction	5
Copulation	95
costs	23, 25

D

Description	13, 93
diet	49
Drop	5

E

Ectothermic	5
Egg Laying	95

F

Feeding	6, 28, 52, 53, 54, 94
Fuzzy	6

G

Gestation Period	6, 95
Glossary	5, 3
Gravid	6

H

habitat	7, 40, 94
handling	63, 65
Hatching	7, 80
Health Conditions	14, 37, 56, 83, 84, 93
Heating Requirements	5, 44, 46
How Many Green Tree Pythons Should You Keep?	5, 21
How Much Does it Cost to Keep a Green Tree Python?	5, 23
How to Choose a Reputable Green Python Breeder	5, 33
Husbandry	7, 27, 39, 57
Hygrometer	7, 48
hypoallergenic	27

I

Incubation	7, 79, 95
Mating	6, 75

L

Laying Eggs	6, 77
Length	13, 93
Length at Birth	95
license or permit	5, 19
Lifespan	14, 93
Lighting Requirements	5, 45

M

Maintaining Humidity	6, 47
Morph	8

N

Necrotic Stomatitis	7, 84, 89
nesting box	77

O

Obvious weight loss	56
Origin and Distribution	5, 12, 14
Other Names	13, 92
overfeeding	55
Oviparous	8
Ovulation and Pre-Lay Shed	6, 76, 95

P

Paper towels	59

Parasites	7, 84, 89
Pinkie	8
Popping	8, 72
Possible Feeding Problems	6, 56
Pre-killed prey storage	50, 54
Primary Behavioral Characteristics	14, 93
Primary Diet	94
Primary Habitat	13, 92
Probing	8
Pros and Cons for the Green Tree Python	26, 27
purchasing	29, 31, 36

R

Recommended Day/Light Cycle	45, 94
Recommended Equipment	94
Recommended Humidity Levels	94
Rectal Prolapse	7, 84, 86
regurgitation	56
Refusal of a meal	56
rescue	24
Respiratory Infections	7, 84, 85
rheostat	48

S

salmonella	28
sanitation	28
Serpentine Locomotion	9
Sexing	6, 72
shedding	9, 58, 70
Spinal Kinks	7, 84, 87
Spot cleaning	58
Summary of Green Tree Python Facts	5, 12

T

Tag	9

Tail-hanging	7, 84, 88
teeth	28
temperament	6, 27, 28, 63, 64
Terrarium	9, 27
Terrarium cleaning	58, 59
Thermal Cycling	6, 74, 95
thermometer	48
thermostat	48
Thermoregulation	9, 40, 41
timer	48

U

F/T	6
Useful Tools and Devices	6, 47, 48

V

Vent	9
Vivarium	9

W

warming	53
Water	94
Water Blisters	7, 84, 90
WC	9
Weaner	9
Weight	13, 93
Weight at Birth	95

Y

Yearling	10

Z

Zoonosis   10

Photo Credits

Page 1 Photo by Ltshears via Wikimedia Commons. <https://commons.wikimedia.org/wiki/File:Green_Tree_Python.jpg>

Page 11 Photo by Fotografiert von Marcel Burkhard alias cele4 via Wikimedia Commons. <https://commons.wikimedia.org/wiki/File:Gruene_baumpython.jpg>

Page 17 Photo by Mike Wesemann Mwx via Wikimedia Commons. <https://commons.wikimedia.org/wiki/File:BaumpythonFarbwechsel.jpg>

Page 29 Photo by Johnkentucky via Wikimedia Commons. <https://commons.wikimedia.org/wiki/File:JBR_7494.jpg>

Page 39 Photo by Foto-Rabe via Pixabay. <https://pixabay.com/en/snake-toxic-green-tree-snake-653649/>

Page 49 Photo by skeeze via Pixabay. <https://pixabay.com/en/green-tree-python-snake-macro-close-1416338/>

Page 57 Photo by 5STARVAs via Pixabay. <https://pixabay.com/en/australian-green-tree-python-python-1099923/>

Page 63 Photo by Ian Chien via Wikimedia Commons. <https://commons.wikimedia.org/wiki/File:Morelia_viridis.jpg>

Page 71 Photo by Haplochromis via Wikimedia Commons. <https://commons.wikimedia.org/wiki/File:Morelia_viridis.JPG>

Page 83 Photo by Pixel-mixer via Pixabay. <https://pixabay.com/en/green-tree-python-snake-non-toxic-942685/>

Page 91 Photo by divinitari via Pixabay. <https://pixabay.com/en/snake-green-tree-python-reptile-1225370/>

References

"Adoptions." Green Tree Python Rescue. <http://greentreepython.org/adoptions.html>

"Breeding Green Tree Pythons." Green Tree Pythons Australia. <http://www.greentreepythonsaustralia.com/breeding.html>

"Breeding Green Tree Pythons (Morelia Viridis). Greg Maxwell. <http://www.reptilesmagazine.com/Breeding-Snakes/Green-Tree-Python-Breeding/>

"Chondro Myth #4: They Can Be Tamed By Handling." Gtpfan. <http://www.gtpfan.com/chondro-myth-4-they-can-be-tamed-by-handling/>

"Choosing a Pet Snake." Lianne McLeod, DVM. <http://exoticpets.about.com/cs/snakes/a/snakesaspets.htm>

"Conquer the Challenge of Breeding Green Tree Pythons." Rico Walder. <http://www.reptilesmagazine.com/Snakes/Breeding-Snakes/Breed-Green-Tree-Pythons/>

"Exotic Pets." Lauren Slater. <http://ngm.nationalgeographic.com/2014/04/exotic-pets/slater-text>

"FAQ's." Allchondros.com.
<http://www.allchondros.com/faq.htm>

"Feeding Your Snake." PetSmart.
<http://pets.petsmart.com/guides/snakes/feeding.shtml>

"Finding a reputable snake breeder online." PetSnakes.com.
<http://pet-snakes.com/finding-reputable-snake-breeder-online>

"Glossary." The Reptilian.co.uk.
<http://www.thereptilian.co.uk/the_reptilian_glossary.html>

"Glossary of Herpetological Terms." RatSnake Foundation.
<http://www.ratsnakefoundation.org/index.php/glossary-of-herpetological-terms>

"Green Tree/Chondro Python Care Sheet." Morelia Pythons.
<http://www.moreliapythons.co.za/greentreepythons_caresheet.php>

"Green Tree Python." LLLReptile.
<https://www.lllreptile.com/articles/64-green-tree-python/>

"Green Tree Python." Australian Reptile Park.
<http://reptilepark.com.au/animals/reptiles/snakes/python/green-tree-python/>

"Green Tree Python." Snake Type.
<http://www.snaketype.com/green-tree-python/>

"Green Tree Python." The Animal Files. <http://www.theanimalfiles.com/reptiles/snakes/python_green_tree.html>

"Green Tree Python." Utah's Hogle Zoo. <https://www.hoglezoo.org/meet_our_animals/animal_finder/green_tree_python/>

"Green Tree Python." Wikipedia. <https://en.wikipedia.org/wiki/Green_tree_python>

"Green Tree Python Care." Rico Walder. <http://www.reptilesmagazine.com/Snake-Care/Green-Tree-Pythons/>

"Green Tree Python Care and Breeding Information." Reptile Community. <http://www.reptile-community.com/smf/index.php?topic=24654.0>

"Green Tree Python Care Sheet." Rico Walder and Trooper Walsh. <http://www.reptilesmagazine.com/Care-Sheets/Snakes/Green-Tree-Python/>

"Green Tree Python Care Sheet." Francly Corns & Chondros. <http://www.franclycac.com/Greentreepythoncaresheet.htm>

"Green Tree Python Care Sheet." Gecko Care. <http://geckocare.net/green-tree-python-care-sheet/>

"Green Tree Python Habitat – Part 1: Heating and Temperature." Reptile Knowledge.

<http://www.reptileknowledge.com/news/green-tree-python-habitat/>

"Green Tree Python Information." Wallflower Herpetoculture. <http://wallflowerherps.weebly.com/green-tree-python-care.html>

"Green Tree Python (Morelia Viridis) Care." Greg Maxwell. <http://www.reptilesmagazine.com/Snake-Care/Green-Tree-Python-Husbandry/>

"Green Tree Pythons Not For Beginners." GTPfan. <http://www.gtpfan.com/green-tree-pythons-not-for-beginners/>

"Green Tree Pythons – Pros and Cons." Right Pet. <https://rightpet.com/reptile/green-tree-python/reviews/3459>

"GTP Husbandry." GTPA. <http://greentreepythonsaustralia.com/husbandry.html>

"Habitats: Cleaning and Disinfecting Reptile Cages." PetEducation.com. <http://www.peteducation.com/article.cfm?c=17+1796&aid=2847>

"Health Issues with GTPs." M. Cermak. <http://www.greentreepythonsaustralia.com/health.html>

"How Do Snakes Maintain Homeostasis?" Pets on Mom.Me. <http://animals.mom.me/snakes-maintain-homeostasis-8859.html>

"How Much Does a Green Tree Python Cost?" howmuchisit.org. <http://www.howmuchisit.org/green-tree-python-cost/>

"How to Bathe a Snake." Cuteness Pets Editor. <https://www.cuteness.com/article/bathe-snake>

"How to Bathe a Snake." PetSnakes.com. <http://pet-snakes.com/bathe-snake>

"How to Buy Your First Green Tree Python." gtpfan. <http://www.gtpfan.com/how-to-buy-your-first-green-tree-python/>

"How to Choose Your First Pet Snake." PetHelpful. <https://pethelpful.com/reptiles-amphibians/Choosing-Your-First-Pet-Snake>

"How to Clean a Snake Cage Quickly and Easily." Reptile Knowledge. <http://www.reptileknowledge.com/news/how-to-clean-a-snake-cage-quickly-and-easily/>

"Husbandry for Boas & Pythons." Avian and Exotic Animal Care. <http://www.avianandexotic.com/care-sheets/reptiles/husbandry-for-boas-pythons/>

"Looking for a Pet Reptile? Consider a Breeder." Erik J. Martin. <http://www.reptilesmagazine.com/Looking-for-a-Pet-Reptile-Consider-a-Breeder/>

"Morelia Viridis Green Tree Python." Animal Diversity Web. <http://animaldiversity.org/accounts/Morelia_viridis/>

"Morelia Viridis Green Tree Python." Encyclopedia of Life. <http://eol.org/pages/962816/hierarchy_entries/41237837/details#behavior>

"Nutrition: Boas and Pythons." Exotic Pet Vet. <http://www.exoticpetvet.net/reptile/snake.html>

"Pet Snakes for Sale – What to Do *Before* You Buy." Brandon Cornett. <http://www.reptileknowledge.com/care/pet-snakes.php>

"Pythonidae." Wikipedia. <https://en.wikipedia.org/wiki/Pythonidae>

"Read this First." Snake Ranch. <http://www.snakeranch.com.au/buying-a-reptile/read-this-first/>

"Reptile Tank Heating and Lighting Guide." Instructables. <http://www.instructables.com/id/Reptile-tank-heating-and-lighting-guide/?ALLSTEPS>

"Snake." Wikipedia. <https://en.wikipedia.org/wiki/Snake>

"Snake Care Guide." LoveThatPet. <https://www.lovethatpet.com/small-pets/snakes/>

"Snake Habitats, How to Create." Doctors Foster and Smith. <http://www.drsfostersmith.com/PIC/Article.cfm?d=157&category=630&articleid=2383>

"So you think you want a pet snake?" robinsfyi.com. <http://www.robinsfyi.com/animals/herps/soyouwantasnake.htm>

"So, you think you want a reptile?" Melissa Kaplan's Herp Care Collection. <http://www.anapsid.org/parent.html>

"Summary of State Laws Relating to Private Possession of Exotic Animals." Born Free USA. <http://www.bornfreeusa.org/b4a2_exotic_animals_summary.php>

"The History of the Mysterious Green Tree Python." XYZ Reptiles. <http://www.xyzreptiles.com/the-history-of-the-mysterious-green-tree-python/>

"The real cost of keeping a snake." PetSnakes.com. <http://pet-snakes.com/cost-of-keeping-a-snake>

"Thermoregulation." Natural History Collection, The University of Edinburgh. <http://www.nhc.ed.ac.uk/index.php?page=24.134.137.139>

"What it Costs to Own a Reptile." Pet Place. <http://www.petplace.com/article/reptiles/general/adopting-or-purchasing-a-reptile/what-it-costs-to-own-a-reptile>

"Which Exotic Pets Are Legal in the United States?" Melissa A. Smith. <https://pethelpful.com/exotic-pets/Where-are-Exotic-Pets-Legal>

Feeding Baby
Cynthia Cherry
978-1941070000

Axolotl
Lolly Brown
978-0989658430

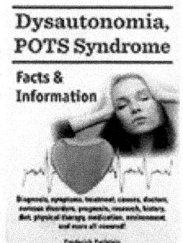

Dysautonomia, POTS Syndrome
Frederick Earlstein
978-0989658485

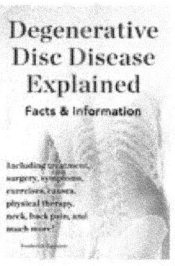

Degenerative Disc Disease Explained
Frederick Earlstein
978-0989658485

Sinusitis, Hay Fever,
Allergic Rhinitis Explained
Frederick Earlstein
978-1941070024

Wicca
Riley Star
978-1941070130

Zombie Apocalypse
Rex Cutty
978-1941070154

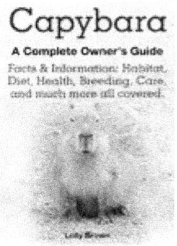

Capybara
Lolly Brown
978-1941070062

Eels As Pets
Lolly Brown
978-1941070167

Scabies and Lice Explained
Frederick Earlstein
978-1941070017

Saltwater Fish As Pets
Lolly Brown
978-0989658461

Torticollis Explained
Frederick Earlstein
978-1941070055

Kennel Cough
Lolly Brown
978-0989658409

Physiotherapist, Physical Therapist
Christopher Wright
978-0989658492

Rats, Mice, and Dormice As Pets
Lolly Brown
978-1941070079

Wallaby and Wallaroo Care
Lolly Brown
978-1941070031

Bodybuilding Supplements
Explained
Jon Shelton
978-1941070239

Demonology
Riley Star
978-19401070314

Pigeon Racing
Lolly Brown
978-1941070307

Dwarf Hamster
Lolly Brown
978-1941070390

Cryptozoology
Rex Cutty
978-1941070406

Eye Strain
Frederick Earlstein
978-1941070369

Inez The Miniature Elephant
Asher Ray
978-1941070353

Vampire Apocalypse
Rex Cutty
978-1941070321

www.ingramcontent.com/pod-product-compliance
Lightning Source LLC
Chambersburg PA
CBHW061447040426
42450CB00007B/1248